Building a Natya Shastra: Individual Voices in an Evolving Public Memory

by

Anandi Leela Devaki Salinas

Department of Religion
Duke University

Date:_____

Approved:

_____

Leela Prasad, Supervisor

_____

David Morgan

_____

Purnima Shah

Thesis submitted in partial fulfillment of
the requirements for the degree of Master of Arts in the Department of
Religion in the Graduate School
of Duke University

2011

UMI Number: 1492181

Dissertation Publishing

ProQuest LLC
789 East Eisenhower Parkway
P.O. Box 1346
Ann Arbor, MI 48106-1346

ABSTRACT

Building a Natya Shastra: Individual Voices in an Evolving Public Memory

by

Anandi Leela Devaki Salinas

Department of Religion
Duke University

Date:_____
Approved:

_____
Leela Prasad, Supervisor

_____
David Morgan

_____
Purnima Shah

An abstract of a thesis submitted in partial
fulfillment of the requirements for the degree
of Master of Arts in the Department of
Religion in the Graduate School
of Duke University

2011

Abstract

In this project, I reassess fundamental assumptions about tradition, classicality, and authenticity by exploring how artists of various Indian dance forms construct and engage these terms in the retelling of the history of their dance styles. To explore the nuances in the negotiation of terminology in the creation of oral histories, as well as to showcase the dancing itself, I have chosen to look at both dance and narrative in multiple formats of video and text. This paper serves both to survey the ethnographic process of making the film as well as to further explore the theoretical possibilities that were evoked in the many narrations in the film. I will eventually suggest that the formulations of classicality and authenticity in relation to text and temple point to the importance of concept of public memory in the creation of a dynamically constituted tradition rooted in foundational texts such as the *Nāṭya Śāstra* and living traditions connected to dance lineages and teachers.

Dedication

mama pitre

Contents

1. Stories

> Let me tell you a story. I grew up in the cultural city of Madras, where I learned bharathanatyam, a form of South Indian classical dance, from a very young age. My dance teachers told me a story, a story they were never tired of repeating... In time, this story became my own, until it was no longer a "story" to me. (Meduri 1988, 1-2)

Even from my brief foray into the field of ethnography, I have noticed that introductory conversations always begin with a story. This story can be a mix of memory, history, and engaging narrative and, in my experience there are often too many layers within a story to analyze while I am simply listening. Many times during long stretches of listening and watching interviews I would hear interesting moments of self-reflection on a topic, something that would be compelling to pursue more in depth. Oddly enough, the premises of these moments are often left untouched and only the germane sound bites are quoted or edited into a final product. I have used my interest in the practice, theory, and history of classical Indian dance forms as the basis for many course papers and have listened to many stories told by dancers, teachers, academics, and students concerning the art during my time as a dancer, but have never actually listened to the frame the stories were told in. Conversations on devotion, for example, would begin by discussing the specific history – a lineage that a dancer or instructor belongs to and their history of that style. To anchor such a history, interwoven through these conversations would be terms such as *tradition, classical,* and *authenticity*; mentioned as if in passing we had all already agreed to what these terms meant to all of us, myself as a dancer included.

In this project, I reassess fundamental assumptions about tradition, classicality, and authenticity by exploring how artists of various Indian dance forms construct and engage these terms in the retelling of the history of their dance styles. To explore the nuances in the negotiation of terminology in the creation of oral histories, as well as to showcase the dancing

1

itself, I have chosen to look at both dance and narrative in multiple formats of video and text. Previously I had filmed another documentary—also on Indian dance—entitled *Why We Dance*, which was created alongside a paper of the same title for a course on ethnography of religion. In that project, I found that exploring narratives in the visual as well as textual domain allows the audience of both the video and text the possibility to experience a more textured connection to the story of the dancer. By exploring narratives in this way, the choices that are made in an interview in terms of questions asked and trajectories of answers allow for a different kind of analysis, one that I would argue aides in exploring assumptions underlining the frameworks of these stories.

This side-by-side exploration of narratives in film and analysis in text is the foundation for this project as well, but instead of focusing on only specific practices assumed to connect to some kind historical context, I began to look at what that context actually is. Rather than moving on past the introductory topics of a conversation, I began to ask dancers to elaborate on that introduction – to tell me the history of their specific dance form as they learned it and which parts of that history they felt spoke the most to the way they practice that art. If a term like *classical* or *tradition* was introduced, I would ask what exactly that term meant to them and how that term fit actively into their practice. Often dancers would say that they or their teachers tried to keep the dance authentic over time and in response I would ask: How do you keep it authentic? What does it mean to be authentic? Many of the dancers would respond with some lighthearted laughter along the lines of: 'That's an interesting question' or 'That is difficult [to answer].' It should not be assumed that dancers regularly sit down to think about the labels that are applied to their art forms or how they themselves perceive the authenticity of their art. Some do, but many do not. The interview format and the questions themselves were meant to mark out an area in which these dancers could try to articulate their feelings on these subjects. Within even one school of dance dedicated to one specific teacher, dancers would respond with a variety of connections and histories, but these histories would all be bounded by distinct references to sources of authenticity, tradition (e.g. teacher lineages, long-standing temple connections, etc.), and underlying requirements and desires to be 'classical.' The results of this approach made me rethink the ways these dance forms are often categorized as 'classical' or 'fusion' (insinuating the inauthentic) and even more fundamentally, how I approached the basic, but complex topic of history in this context of oral narratives that include allegiances to teachers and texts.

To highlight the narratives and the actual dance movements (which, by the end of this paper, I will argue are another form of dialogue in the negotiation of a history) this project is equally spread across the multiple media, specifically, the narratives existing in the film and the analysis of the film's themes, along with some traditional ethnographic transcription, in the paper. The ethnographic film focuses on individual reflections on 'tradition', 'classicality', and 'authenticity' from nine dancers, instructors, performers, and enthusiasts as a kind of 'visual oral histories' project. This paper serves both to survey the ethnographic process of making the film as well as to further explore the theoretical possibilities that were evoked in the many narrations in the film. I will eventually suggest that the formulations of classicality and authenticity in relation to text and temple point to the importance of the concept of public memory in the creation of a dynamically constituted tradition, which is rooted in foundational texts such as the *Nāṭya Śāstra* and living traditions connected to dance lineages and teachers. The title *Building a Natya Shastra* is a reference to the ancient Sanskrit treatise on dramaturgy and aesthetic theory, but in this case it can literally mean: building a 'science of dance.' The presence of the term *Nāṭya Śāstra*, commonly referred to by dancers as one of the origins of Indian dance forms, links the context to a specific kind of authoritative past and to notions of classicality and authenticity, and to me signifies the ongoing engagement and creation of pasts. The title is then a kind of example of the multi-faceted nature of history in Indian dance. The *Nāṭya Śāstra* was composed thousands of

3

years ago, but what matters more than what exists in the text is how the *idea* of such a text is used and how the science of classical Indian dance is being constantly rebuilt.

2. Classical, Authenticity, and Tradition: Fundamental Markers of a History

For this two-part project, I wanted to interview dancers from as many different styles of Indian dance as possible. By the end of the two-month interview window[1], I was able to interview friends and dancers in several styles that I have also practiced – *bhārata nāṭyam, āndhra nāṭyam, oḍiśī* – plus a few visiting artists of these styles from India and Los Angeles while being based entirely in the triangle region of North Carolina. The dance forms that I was able to document were only a consequence of being constrained to an area where these styles were prevalent.[2] Many of the dancers I interviewed I had previously danced with, some I was currently in a performance group with, and others I had only just met and had only one hour to talk to them on account of their busy schedules.

Before continuing onto the topic of terminology, I would like to provide a brief background to the kinds of dance forms that are the focus of this project. So far I have been referring to these dances forms simply as types of Indian dance, however, Indian dance is not a singular art form and even using the term 'Indian dance' assumes a kind of linearity and umbrella definition of the dance forms. Having to start from somewhere, in everyday conversation, Indian dance forms are generally categorized into several types of dance from the subcontinent that are labeled as classical, folk, and perhaps even a sub-genre of folk that includes Bollywood-inspired forms. For this project, because of limitations of time and resources I have had to restrict myself to only three of the eight dances that the Sangeet Natak Akademi in New Delhi[3] has defined as

---

[1] I rented equipment for this project from the Duke OIT department, which limits the time lengths of film equipment rentals. The equipment rental process was another limitation of the scope of the filming portion of this project.
[2] I made some attempts to contact Kathak dancers, a style from north India, but no one responded. The time and travel limitations were incredibly apparent, but even with the smaller sample of styles, I feel that the questions I had were fully represented in just a few dance styles or even within a single style.
[3] The Sangeet Natak Akademi is a national academy for arts and part of a governmental institution that oversees cultural affairs.

'classical' – *bhārata nāṭyam, āndhra nāṭyam*, and *oḍiśī*.[4] Unfortunately by following what has become the standard terminology of the art, I am already allowing the assumption of classicality to go somewhat unquestioned. However, although I focus on forms that are already popularly understood to be 'classical,' this distinction also confers forms of special treatment that these arts receive nationally and internationally on account of the way their styles have been perceived by governmental, national, and international institutions and individuals. More fundamentally, my project seeks to explore what exactly is understood as constituting the classicality of these dance styles, given that in the absence of a cohesive or definitive statement of what makes a dance classical many dancers have created their own standards of classicality. Within contemporary schools and 'classical' dance groups, the understanding of the terms *tradition, classical,* and *authenticity* are many times ingrained so deeply into the definitions of their forms that self-reflection on *why* the dance is considered as classical, *what* tradition means in this context, and *what* exactly does it mean to be authentic – are rarely priorities.

Bhārat nāṭyam is argued, and lamented by some, as the most popular classical Indian dance form on the global stage, and even perhaps as the prime example of classical dance in India to which other dance forms are measured in their attainment of classical status (Shah 2002, 138). The dance form hails from the south Indian state of Tamil Nadu and has been the subject of countless academic studies (Soneji 2010, O'Shea 2008, Weidman 2006, Allen 1997, Gaston 1996, Meduri 1988, Kersenboom-Story 1987, to mention a few). Without attempting to provide a normalizing historical narrative of the dance, *bhārat nāṭyam* has existed as a classical Indian dance only since the early twentieth century – revived, reconstituted, reinvented, and recreated in light of a temple-related form known as *sadir*. Early twentieth century backlash against forms of

---

[4] It should be noted that the criteria by which a form is labeled as such has never actually been released by the Akademi (Shah 2002, 2010).

dance associated with temples across India was in large part due to the associations made by elite social and political figures of dancers with prostitution and marriages of young girls to temple deities (O'Shea 2008, Meduri 1988). Matthew Allen gives a general sense, although historically decontextualized, of a kind of 'classical' (i.e. standard) definition of a temple dancer :

> Devadasis (dasi, servant, of deva, god) were female Hindu ritual practitioners, women who underwent training and initiation in religious-artistic service, including dance and vocal music. After her period of training, a devadasi was ritually married to the god of a Hindu temple and therefore became nityasumangali, always-auspicious, by virtue of the fact that, married to the god, she could never become a widow. (Allen 1997, 65)

In addition to being married to a deity, the 'traditional' *devadāsī* was kept apart from the public, as was her dance. What Allen does not mention is that while this was the typical definition of a temple dancer, historical factors such as waning of state patronage for many regional dance styles would change the ways in which temples, and thus their dancers, were funded. In the early twentieth century, Dr. Muthulakshmi Reddy lead a large initiative to eradicate the *devadāsī* tradition in south India (ramifications would be felt throughout India for all temple dancer communities) by linking the contemporary dancers of the time to a corrupted version of the "always-auspicious" dancers who did not mingle with the public, let alone take on patrons or have children. Saskia Kerseboom-Story quotes the preamble of the "Devadasi Act," which ended the formal practice of the *devadāsī* and eventually passed in November 1947, though the social stigma of the association with temple dancers began much earlier:

> Whereas the practice still prevails in certain parts of the Province of Madras of dedicating women as "devadasis" to Hindi deities, idols, objects of worship, temples and other religious institutions. And whereas such practice, however ancient and pure in its origin, leads many of the women so dedicated to a life of prostitution; and whereas it is necessary to put an end to the practice...(Government of Madras, Law Department, G.O. No. 23, January 26, 1948 Acts; quoted in Kersenboom-Story 1987, xxi)

These associations were looked down upon by the new colonial social standards of the period and for temple dances to continue at all, they would have to be reinvented as dances that would appeal to a mass audience of this new social standard. In the case of *bhārata nāṭyam*, Rukmini Devi, a brahmin, western-educated woman, was the main figure associated with 'reviving' the style, applying standardizing techniques reminiscent of western classical dances such as ballet (interestingly enough, many of the dancers who I interviewed compare their forms to ballet in terms of how classical or serious they are). Other styles across India were born in similar ways, each creation/recreation based on a pre-colonial period form, and many were systematized and deemed classical only in the last 50 to 75 years. The styles of *āndhra nāṭyam* and *oḍiśī* are among these younger forms, both hailing from the eastern parts of India, Andhra Pradesh and Orissa, respectively. Both forms were associated with temple dances prior to their revival and also credit a single or group of teachers with the revival of these art forms.

What was often key in terms of these revivals was the goal of associating these newly crafted forms with the idea of classicality as is understood in the modern western sense of being authoritative, traditional, and serious. The Oxford English Dictionary defines *classical* as it pertains to arts as "representing an exemplary standard; traditional and long-established in form or style" (Oxford English Dictionary 2010, "classical"). During the early twentieth century, music in India was also undergoing similar shifts to 'classical' standards and this shift has spawned significant literature on the classicality of Indian music during this period. Janaki Bakhle, in her book *Two Men and Music*, summarizes the milieu for performing arts in India at this time. For some music scholars, Bakhle writes, "classicization meant at least two things: system, order, discipline, and theory, on the one hand, and antiquity of national origin, on the other" (Bakhle 2005, 124; also in Dennen 2010, 162). This form of "system, order, discipline, and theory" was modeled on western forms of classical music and was adapted to pre-existing indigenous art

8

forms in both music and dance by various groups of western and high-caste Indian artists and enthusiasts (Allen 1997, Bakhle 2005, Weidman 2006). In the case of *oḍiśī* music, David Dennen lists three criteria generally used to argue for the music from the state of Orissa to be considered classical, which I believe could be easily generalized as describing many music and dance traditions in my experience: "the argument of antiquity, the argument of systematicness, and the argument of distinctiveness" (Dennen 2010, 164). Beginning with the third argument for classical status, distinctiveness is what sets the art form apart from others both in India and in the west. Weidman, in her discussion of south Indian classical music, argues that it is the vocal tradition within that genre that lends to it its distinctiveness and in turn authenticity and tradition (Weidman 2006, 8). *Bhārata nāṭyam, āndhra nāṭyam,* and *oḍiśī* are often described by their proponents as having unique or distinctive features against western dance and are described as having many dimensions of facial expressions, technique, and dramatic elements as opposed to western styles that have only technique or drama. Indian dance forms are also posed against each other – *oḍiśī* and its torso movements, *āndhra nāṭyam* and its changing levels and singing/lip-syncing, and *bhārata nāṭyam* and its strict angular technique and adherence to lines – and these distinct features are many times tied to descriptions in ancient texts or to postures sculpted on centuries-old temple walls.

The first two arguments can be linked, in the case of Indian dance, because antiquity and "systematicness" (or as Dennen specifies, the "scientificness", Dennen 2010, 164) are often brought together through connections to texts. The connections frequently made by dancers and scholars of Indian dance to authenticity and "systematicness" reveal textual evidence for their specific dance style. These textual citations often link traditions to works on aesthetics in the Sanskritic tradition, notably the *Nāṭya Śāstra* (a text from approximately 200 c.e.) and the *Abhinaya Darpana* (18th century, Shah 2002, 134) – although regional texts in regional languages are also cited. Purnima Shah, in her article on the creation of "classical," regional Indian dance forms writes on the usage of the term "classical:"

> There is no synonym for the Western term "classical" in either Sanskrit or Hindi, which does not mean that such a concept as "classical" does not exist in India, but its usage is not quite the same. The meaning and equivalent term used for the purpose of translation is shastriya, literally meaning "textual," or pertaining to the shastras (texts). In that sense, the term "classical" dance would translate as dance pertaining to the shastras and hence inclusive of the oral tradition to the extent of its inclusivity in the shastras. Although the gurus who trained disciples in these art forms were informed by the shastras, the actual training was passed on from the guru to the disciple through an oral tradition... In the term shastriya, therefore, lies the classicism of the dance as we see it celebrated in the national dance festivals with all the regalia, glamor, and dazzle that transcends the present and transports the audience to a desired past. (Shah 2002, 137)

A connection to a *śāstra*, defined as "order, command, precept, or rule" (Monier Williams Online) creates a link to an outside validating force that has time and a socially authoritative standing on its side. The authorial character of a *śāstra* is often times included within the textual work itself. Leela Prasad writes of the *Nāṭya Śāstra*: "In the encyclopedic [text], Bharata [the purported author of *the Nāṭya Śastra*] declares that we need shastras because, unlike divine creation, the human creative act calls for regulation" (Prasad 2007, 102). The authoritativeness of a text such as the *Nāṭya Śāstra* comes from a connection to Vedic texts (the *Nāṭya Śāstra* is in good company as one of many texts that claims to be the 'fifth Veda,' an elusive external text to the canonical four Vedas) and internal references to divine composition. Prasad writes that the *Nāṭya Śāstra* "imagines itself as a 'shastra of *prayoga*,' a theory of praxis " (Prasad 2007, 100), and thus is prescriptive by design. The *Nāṭya Śāstra*, in its fourth and ninth book contains detailed descriptions of postures, stances, hand gestures, and general attitude and appearance of a kind of Indian dance that pre-dates any kind of categorization (indigenous or otherwise). It is not necessarily a question of whether or not the dance forms of the contemporary period in India actually follow these prescriptions to the letter when they invoke connections to the *Nāṭya Śāstra*. It can be argued that the very definition of a *śāstra* includes not only its strict prescriptions but also debate and fluidity over its impact on practice. Prasad, in her study on daily ethics in a town in the south Indian state of Karnataka, writes on the fluidity of such concrete texts:

> Conversational narratives in Sringeri reveal that, although historically traced to millennia-old Sanskrit texts [*śāstra*] and manipulated to a great degree by colonial administrators, shastra is in everyday life a nebulous but dynamic and open-ended cultural background that influences conceptualizations of conduct and is in turn influenced by them. (Prasad 2007, 118)

Reflecting on the everyday connection to *śāstras* in use, Prasad continues: "Despite the fact that a rule may be defined with some precision in the shastras or in the sampradaya [tradition] (or any normative body), 'its' meaning emerges in the practice itself" (135). Ultimately, she finds that *śāstra* functions as an 'imagined text,' contextually constructed and expressed within its own set of accountabilities. The precedent for following specific *śāstric* rules becomes itself a kind of ongoing tradition. This kind of tradition that draws on practice and text is constantly in conversation with itself as new circumstances require reevaluation of *śāstra*. The 'tradition' referred to by many of the dancers in the film reflects more than just *śāstric* definitions of dance postures. These invocations of tradition generally refer to years of practice and generations of teachers and students that adhere to certain guidelines for their practice and the sense of continuing the prescriptions of *Nāṭya Śāstra*. In contemporary dance, these teachers of the lineage, or traditions of dance, adhere to the kind of strictly outlined systematic method of teaching and performing created in response to the calls for classicization of Indian dance in the early twentieth century. The history frequently referred to in this project – a *classical* history of 'classical' Indian dance – includes all of these elements – textuality, lineage, and the tradition of following a specific teacher's style of dance (sometimes includes of philosophy and devotion). Because this 'history' seems to be so individualistic, rethinking how we compose our questions about history and narrative would allow scholars to move beyond single-sided history mapping when discussing Indian dance communities.

In an edited volume entitled *Oral Histories and Public Memories*, the editors argue that the strict use of either only oral histories or memory studies will exclude vital aspects of academic studies. The use of only either oral histories, which focuses on the individual, or memory studies, which are argued to be inherently social, will leave out either socio-political power dynamics that have helped form the memory in the former, or leave out the agency and the lived aspects of the memories in the latter (Hamilton and Shopes 2008, x-xi). However, the use of these together can help strike a balance of focus. The editors quote Barbara Misztal as arguing that, "In order for the notion of memory to be a useful analytical concept we need to retain a sense of both its individual and collective dimensions" (xi). Christian Lee Novetzke, writing about the 13th-14th century Bhakti saint from Western India, Namdev, has used the popular ideas of 'publics' and memory studies to describe a continuous reflection and recreation of notions of devotion within the tradition. Novetzke writes:

> [T]he ubiquitous religiosocial category of *bhakti*, or "devotion," in India that surrounds Namdev is best understood neither as a "*bhakti* movement" nor "personal devotion" but, rather, as an ongoing effort to construct publics of belief, maintained through intricate systems of memory that surround Namdev and the publics that maintain, and are sustained by, that memory. (Novetzke 2008, xi)

Novetzke's brief summary on the connection between the individual and the social, the past and the present, to me mirrors the same kind of connection between these poles within the Indian dance forms. As is the case with Namdev in Novetzke's study, the Indian dance forms here are perhaps better described in terms of publics that create and recreate a kind of memory in a public sphere that recalls connections to institutions of temple dance and *śāstric* authority. Before moving into the narratives and Novetzke's public memory framework applied to this case, I will outline the visual ethnographic project and discuss some of the general issues involved in making this ethnographic film.

3. Authority in the Ethnographic Film Process Revisited

The ethnographic film project began in September 2010 and interviews were conducted up to November 2010. The editing process took approximately two months and resulted in a 45-minute final film. During the course of filming, I was able to conduct 12 half-hour to hour-long interviews with professional dancers, dance students, teachers, and enthusiasts living in or visiting the central North Carolina area. On some occasions I was also allowed to film some of their professional performances and workshop sessions. In many cases, I asked dancers to supply me with dance footage from their own personal collections, and if footage was unavailable directly from the dancers, I collected performance footage available on personal websites or YouTube. My previous film, *Why We Dance*, was created in a very different manner and the lessons in ethnographic authority from that process have greatly influenced the construction, execution, and analysis of narratives for this project. The basis for that film was taken from topics in a course on ethnography and religion and its purpose was to engage issues in the ethnographic process in a visual medium. The film was quite different in scope in that I followed one dancer, a close friend of mine, and her burgeoning Indian dance school and new dance students. I have decided to include comparisons to this previous project here to highlight how subtle, even logistical changes in ethnographic decisions can affect the final ethnographic project, and thus the kind and quality of analysis possible with that ethnographic material.

As a basis for that project, I decided to use James Clifford's four ethnographic methods as outlined in his paper *On Ethnographic Authority* and other ethnographic problems such as the insider/outsider position and ethnographic authority in visual media. Of particular interest to me were Clifford's modes of the *dialogic* and the *polyphonic*, ethnographic modes of authority that can visually or textually connect the audience and interviewees through a collaborative authorial engagement with the people in the study. My paper, also entitled *Why We Dance*, went into detail

13

on each of Clifford's ethnographic modes: participatory, interpretive, dialogic, and polyphonic, to give a sense of how I grappled with issues in each authoritative technique.[1] I tried to use that project as an exercise in how to limit my ethnographic authority over the people in my studies and how to make a more well-rounded, collaborative project. *Building a Natya Shastra*, I hoped, would be a similar exercise in expanding the base of such a project to include a wider variety of interviewees and span more dance styles to give more breadth to the film. Instead I was, in many cases, unable to keep up the type of collaborative effort I enjoyed previously – engaging many of the same ethnographic issues but under new circumstances. Without going into too much detail on the ethnographic methods or their limitations and benefits, I will present them as a framework methodology to reflect on this film project in light of my similar, previous visual ethnography project.

In his paper, *On Ethnographic Authority*, James Clifford discusses four ethnographic methodologies – the experiential, interpretive, dialogic, and polyphonic – each of which, if carefully executed, could limit the amount and severity of ethnographic authority over a textual project (Clifford 1983, 142). The experiential mode is one of engagement with the people and activities of a project, often noted as the 'participant-observation' method of ethnography. The interpretive mode is an ethnographic technique that serves to ground the straight experiential description and data and compose it into "a corpus, a potentially meaningful ensemble separated out from an immediate discursive or performative situation. In the moment of textualization this meaningful corpus assumes a more or less stable relation to a context, and we are familiar with the end result of this process in much of what counts as ethnographic thick description" (Clifford 1983, 130-131). The dialogic method seeks to highlight the interactive elements in the

---

[1] Salinas, Anandi. 2009. "Why We Dance: Motivations and Religious Identities in an American Bharata Natyam School" *Ethnography and Religion*. Professor Leela Prasad

ethnographic project by calling attention to actual dialogue through such practices as the transcription of texts in field notes. Finally, the polyphonic mode of ethnography attempts to broaden the authorship of an ethnographic work to include those that make up the project itself. The ways in which authorship is dispersed to contributors depends on the kind of project undertaken by the scholar, but can include a wide range of collaborations including multiple authorship, multiple editors, or even collaboration at the level of creative and dynamic input in the final project.

Clifford's methodologies describe the process of positioning oneself during the creation of an ethnographic text (or in my case, that of a visual text). While locating oneself in relation to interviewees, the ethnographer has to make tangible, very real decisions on their relationships to those in the study that can impact their authority over the project, the topic, the people in the study, and future relationships with those people. The reader (or visual audience) forms a kind of relationship based on trust with the author of a study. For example, the experiential method, based on the long-standing tradition of participant-observation, is easily suited to exerting authority over a study: allowing the voice of the author to override the voices, if any, of the people in the study. Because it is the academic author writing the final paper, and not the informants or people associated with the study, and because of the likelihood that the reader or audience has not been to that location or studied that particular topic, the reader/audience defers authority to one who has the experience. As Clifford writes: "Precisely because it is hard to pin down, 'experience' has served as an effective guarantee of ethnographic authority" (Clifford 1983, 130). Exerting ethnographic authority in a project subdues any presence of the voices of the participants in the study and leaves only the academic voice to make the final point. Clifford's article on the subject of ethnographic authority outlines the limitations and benefits of each method, and concludes that an ethnographic project that negotiates both positive and negative aspects of each ethnographic method, in a collaborative fashion with those in the study, would limit the authority of a singular author. Such an endeavor would provide a study that places the ethnographer and the interviewee/informant/friend on more equal footing.

Although he does not address visual ethnography in his essay, the same issues of authority and negotiation are also applicable in the visual field. In my previous film, I attempted to limit my authority in a number of ways, most of which included expanding the project to be more collaborative. Previous examples included the careful negotiation of the participant-observation model (experiential) in that I was dancing and teaching along with interviewing and filming. During the film editing process, I attempted to pay close attention to contextualizing interviews (interpretive) and the role that visual editing would play on the overall authority of the project. I constantly reviewed the process of filming and the scope of the project with the dancers, asking for feedback frequently, and ensured that our conversations were shown in the final film (dialogic and polyphonic). For this project, I attempted to follow the methods I had previously used for *Why We Dance*, but the scope of *Building a Natya Shastra*, in interview and film length, made it nearly impossible to properly negotiate each of these methods to increase collaboration.

In terms of the experiential method for *Building a Natya Shastra*, I was an active dance participant with many of the dancers in this project during the three months of filming, and in some cases I had previously been a student or dance assistant with other dancers. In the case of Mythili Prakash, however, I had never danced with her or actually seen her dance in person (the televised performance I had seen was a very distant engagement with her dancing). In this project, this experiential methodology could not be so clearly defined as in my previous project where I was literally dancing five minutes before I was filming. In this case, rarely was I dancing along with the interviewees or taking part in joint classes or performances. As a consequence of expanding the project to include more dancers, I did not feel the closeness I had felt with the

16

dancers I interviewed for *Why We Dance*, but because I was still a 'classical' Indian dancer, there was already a baseline "acceptance and empathy" (Clifford 1983, 128) between myself and the famous world-class dancers I had never met before in my life. This existing comfort with a language of Indian dance, specifically those that are labeled as 'classical' (by dancers themselves and by third-parties) allowed me a certain amount of insider identity even with dancers I did not know. I had also discussed the issues that I have faced as a non-Indian dancer interviewing a variety of Indian artists in terms of the insider/outsider positions in my paper, *Why We Dance*. Through both of these projects, I have found that Kirin Narayan's emphasizing of "shifting identifications amid a field of interpenetrating communities and power relations" (Narayan 1993, 671) instead of focusing on the preexisting binary identities fits actual practice of ethnography more than distinct insider/outsider identities. [2] Throughout this project, as in my previous one, the constant movement in the spectrum of insider-outsider scholar/dancer/student/friend/etc. identities was very tangible and a distinct factor in interviews, logistics, and relationships.

During the process of film production for *Why We Dance*, I had analyzed the editing methods I used and concluded that the less manipulation in sound and visual editing, the less authority that I would be imposing on the interpretive ethnographic process. Of course, because I was still analyzing all the interviews and fitting them together in some kind of narrative arc, my interpretive authority was naturally present. I argued that in film ethnography, sound and visual manipulation are actually very difficult for viewers to detect, a negative feature that both textual and visual ethnography share. That film was only 30 minutes long and mainly used one long

---

[2] Margaret Mills, in her work *Rhetoric and Politics in Afghan Traditional Storytelling*, discusses her shifting from "entertainment to interrogation" by conducting interview style sessions and how asking certain questions or simply being present would shift the types of answers she would elicit from her informants versus a man, in her case, would get (Mills 1991, 47). In the case of *Building a Natya Shastra*, my presence as a non-Indian dancer was more complicated than a gender binary because I was raised in an Indian community, thus experienced in the general culture of many households, but also I am a dancer. I do not know whether an Indian dancer would have elicited the same responses from the dancers in this project, but author identity is part of the context of the project, and thus should also be taken into consideration.

interview with a sort of built-in narrative structure. This project, by comparison, with its 12 long interviews (only nine were included in the final version) and different base styles and stories was a much more challenging process that required more careful attentiveness during post-production. Even the very basic fundamental concept of "dryness" was a problem in the initial cuts of the film because there was simply too much uncut talking. Plus, in an hour-long interview, realizations and connections are not made in a nice, easily editable linear fashion. Sound and visual editing were a must for this project, in addition to rearranging interview segments. Even though some of the editing was masked by archival footage, I am still aware that I was forced to shift around interview segments to clarify points and shorten interviews. This kind of editing can be a risky path in terms of limiting authority because of its subtle nature. For my part, I tried to be overly aware of my editing to keep the sense of the statements intact while taking out discussions that were only tangentially related to the topics of the project and interruptions.

There was one specific carryover editing method from my first project – my decision not to provide any voiceover for the project at all. For one, this project is about the multiplicities that exist in the narratives of these art forms, so for me to overlay my voice at the beginning of the film to attempt to explain a simplified history of any of the forms or what classical dance is, would be already placing an expectation of what the stories *should be* or how to interpret them. Peter Loizos describes this approach to film ethnography as an "explanation rejected" method – instead of proposing audio or textual commentary at the outset (or throughout) the film, restraining from such explanation changes the initial reaction of the viewer (Loizos 1992, 57). Loizos uses this mode to describe a film with no commentary or interviews at all, but my project is vastly different in that it is comprised entirely of interviews. The film with no commentary lacks kind of "thick description," while my film of 'thick interviewing' lacks framing and explanatory shots of dance culture. The issue with these projects that lack explanation, is that they are hardly 'texts' in a vacuum and should not necessarily be treated as stand alone studies, but should be paired with a text for further context (Loizos 1992, 58 and footnote). As interesting as it is for me to see so many different dancers come together (even in an imagined visual space) to discuss the histories of their art forms, the film is meant to be paired with a paper, not as an independent film project. If this film were separated from the paper, I would have to include much more background about Indian dance and likely voiceover to describe the purpose of the film. As innocent as these alternatives may seem, because the premise of the project as a whole, including this analysis paper, was to reevaluate what a historical narrative can be, adding an authorial layer of background 'historical' material to separate the paper from the film would have placed the narratives as secondary to an authoritative film introduction. In this film-paper linked fashion, the academic audience could view the film – the narratives by themselves – and then read the paper to go more in depth into the narratives and analytical methods to approach them.

To this end, the solution to the lengthy uncut interviews was to actively use the interviews themselves as voiceovers as much as possible. The dancers, students, and enthusiasts are all given ample speaking time on camera, and it is their voiceovers that provide the narrative to any additional scenes or archival footage. For one of her ethnographic films, Jean Lydall noted that screeners for the film actually asked for more on-camera face time with the interviewees and less voiceover work:

> "Voice off" commentary has something authoritarian about it. One can do all sorts of manipulations with it. It is, as it were, subject to the will of the filmmaker. But when I have someone in front of the camera, a physical person, a speaking body that is something quite different... Once someone has been introduced, it's conceivable that you let them speak "off screen." But "voice off" also has something of commentary about it, it's always a bit like an explanation machine, it always involves some control of the filmmaker over his protagonists...(Bayer et al. 88-9; quoted in Lydall 2008, 44)

Because of time constraints, the more dance footage added to act as examples of dance styles, the more interview time needed to either be voiceover or cut entirely. In the final version of the film, there was still a lot of straight interview footage without many cut scenes and voiceovers. To alleviate my anxiety over having such a discussion-focused film, I decided that the film could actually be seen as a visual version of a traditional ethnography. The stories of this project are at the center of the concept of Indian dance artists as a public, to which I will return shortly, and to this end the film is mainly interviews and lengthy discussion on personal histories of dance. Rather than focusing on innovative and aesthetically pleasing scenes of dancing or explanatory scenes that summarize theoretical points, the film focuses on words and individuals telling stories. Thus the film could actually replace a traditional textual ethnographic transcription and serve as an experiment in alternative ethnographic reference 'texts.' Instead of reading a short excerpt in dialogue or paraphrase form while reading textual analysis on the same subject, the film provides a visual connection to the speaker of the dialogue as well as extra inflection coming directly from the interviewee without relying on textual techniques to render nuance and emphasis.

Reflecting on the entire interpretive process of 'textual' creation, in this case a visual text, it is clear that the actual creation of a visual narrative was the most difficult aspect of the film portion of this project. While trying to give each interviewee enough time and space to express their histories and memories of their dance, I still had to weave all of these narratives together into a cohesive work that illustrated the multiplicities of stories while underlining the connected nature of this public. An ethnographic film on one topic, one narrative, has the added flexibility to construct an overarching narrative for the purpose of telling one story. When there are multiple stories to tell, the process becomes much more difficult. I made the decision early on to separate the interviews by dance style rather than leave them in a random order because while all of the styles, I argue, are somehow linked together, there are important differences in interpretation within each of these sub-communities.

The experiential and interpretive modes are perhaps more naturally inclined to a singular authority because the author does not need to consult with any one of their interviewees to proceed with analysis and interpretation. To ameliorate some of these authority issues, Clifford proposes the final two ethnographic methodologies – the dialogic and the polyphonic (Clifford 1983, 133). The dialogic method seeks to highlight the actual dialogue that occurs in an ethnographic project and, along with the polyphonic/multiple author methods, these modes can widen the authorship of a project while limiting the scholarly authority and singular representative problems with the previous methods. In most ethnographic films that I have seen, and in the documentary genre more broadly, authors/directors are rarely heard actually asking questions in the film. Many film ethnographers tailor their interviews and conversations so that the filmmaker/ethnographer is unheard and their presence minimized in the audio-visual dimension of the film (Levin and Cruz 2008, 62). In this kind of visual ethnography, I feel that the questions that are eliciting the answers on screen should also be available to the viewer to be scrutinized and analyzed along with the rest of the interview and audio-visual decisions. To this end, I left more of my questions in this final film than in my previous project, along with my interjections ("ah," "mmhmm," "yeah"), allowing the segments to take on a more conversational tone. Unlike more 'traditional' textual ethnography, these conversations are marked off by an obvious interview setup and are more like appointments in front of a camera than any insights that might come from more casual discussions. The benefit of this format for this project is that it mirrors the situations in which dancers, students, and enthusiasts have to regularly explain their dance forms. Reflecting on her history with ethnography and Indian dance, Janet O'Shea argues that formatting the ethnography as an interview would also allow for a demarcating of "public and private selves" (O'Shea 2006, 144). In the case of this project, I found this an added benefit to the format, in that the dancers would be sharing with me narratives that were generally available in a public sphere. Dancers, especially teachers, performers, and choreographers in the diaspora, frequently have to publicly summarize their dance form, something of its essence and its history, and these public actions are moments of 'memory performance' that link these dancers together as a 'public,' concepts that I will return to shortly.

Unfortunately, because many of the dancers in this project were incredibly busy traveling and performing, I was unable to discuss the project with them as it developed or include them in the decision making process—something I had accomplished in my earlier film. I was unable to spend time with one particular group, let alone one dancer, and I worried about quantity versus quality of relationships. Yet, because the nature of the collaboration in this film differed from my first film, I was able to reflect on the many ways in which polyphonic authorship can be created in ethnographic media. During the making of this documentary, I requested film clips from dancers that they felt would be appropriate for the project. I also discussed with participants how their interviews, comments, and relevant footage would be used before the film was in the editing phase so that they understood how their input shaped the larger context and direction of the film.

As much as I wanted the film to adhere to the ethnographic process of polyphonic authorship that I had followed in *Why We Dance*, this documentary became a very different kind of collaborative process. The project may have decreased the overall notion of multiple authors, but I have instead put more emphasis on the importance of my level of authorship, particularly in the interpretive space of editing the film. Because logistics and relationships did not allow me to directly follow the outline of my previous film, I was forced to reflect on the dynamic capabilities of each ethnographic mode of authorship. Each method in Clifford's ethnographic toolkit had to not only be acknowledged, but also carefully negotiated and renegotiated. With more time and resources (maybe even a second person to assist in audio and secondary camera work), more

22

complex relationships could be explored and would likely benefit the actual purpose of the project a great deal.

4. Tradition, Classicism, and Authenticity – Mapping Narratives and Histories

Because this project is about Indian dancers and stories of their art forms, I will start off with my own.[1] Unlike Avanthi Meduri, I did not grow up hearing a narrative about Indian dance; I only began to really learn about the art forms under that umbrella term as an adult. Even when I started dancing, my *bhārata nāṭyam* teacher did not give me a history lesson. All I knew about the dance form I had chosen at that time was that it was from south India, it was old, and it was religiously based in terms of performance items and a kind of dance language. As I engaged the art form more seriously as a dancer and then later in the academic context, I began to hear more narratives from other students and teachers. Last year I attended a house lecture by Sunil Kothari on modern 'classical' Indian dance forms that showcased a video of new and experimental forms that, he argued, still retained a connection to an ancient textual base and adherence to systems of movement within every *mudrā* (hand gesture) and every move (Kothari 2009), associations that have come to be connected to socio-aesthetic features of classicism. During one of the interviews for *Why We Dance*, a senior dancer reflected on her current devotional sentiment towards dance as having historical precedent because that style of dance originated in the temples as an act of devotion (Dasmuth 2009). During the summer 2010, I was given the opportunity to see Kavita Dwibedi perform an *oḍiśī* lecture-demonstration at the University of Hyderabad in Hyderabad, Andhra Pradesh. She began her short performance with a brief history of the form and marked this brief introduction in three distinct ways: connection to second century cave depictions in Orissa, connection to the *māhārī/gotipua* dancers, and direct connection to temples via the *māhārīs* and to the very structure of the temple itself (Dwibedi 2010). In my own academic

---

[1] Hopefully the reader will have already watched the ethnographic film so that my story will not affect the reader's interpretation of the narratives of the other dancers!

studies of 'classical' Indian dance, I have heard narratives in the more western tradition of historiography underline the changes of dance forms due to socio-political factors in pre-colonial, colonial, and post-colonial periods, narratives that I had never heard from my own dance teachers. Somehow all of these differing historical narratives describe the same group of 'classical' Indian dance forms, and for myself as a dancer, I am placed in a position to negotiate all of these histories to create my own story.

The dancers, students, and enthusiasts in the *Building a Natya Shastra* film each tell the story of the history of the Indian dance they participate in. Amanda Geroy, Mythili Prakash, and Purnima Shah all question the direct link to an unchanged, ancient art form, but nevertheless they use same terms – *tradition*, *classical*, and *authentic* – to describe the nature and history of their styles. When I asked what it means to identify their form as classical or what it means to retain tradition and authenticity, each provided a different answer, thus suggesting the critical importance of these terms as well as the wide range of meanings associated with them to the understanding of a history of classical Indian dance. Nina Dash, in describing how her school keeps its authenticity intact while being outside of India, says that she relies on the instructors who she brings from India to the United States to help connect her school to the authentic *oḍiśī*. She prefers specific teachers based on the level of 'fusion' elements within their dance training and choreography. Kavitha Konda connects *āndhra nāṭyam* and another regional style of Andhra Pradesh to classicality based on long standing 'traditions' of the dance "passed down from generations to generations" and to those temple dance-based lineages. Ramya Sundaresan Kapadia uses a "serious text," such as the *Nāṭya Śāstra*, to create boundaries for classicism in her choreography and compositions. The Duke Lasya co-captains both describe the movements themselves as being the marker of classicism in their practice and choreography.

25

Western academic literature of each form looks at dates and archeological evidence to build a 'factual' history of each form—end of the story. However, much of the evidence is debatable and many of the dates unverifiable. Even so, to look at these narratives in such a way would be to continue a tradition of scholarship that seeks to propose only one, western interpretation of history over another culture – here an ancient/modern, religious/secular, Indian/global art culture. As a dancer who has been exposed to a multiplicity of histories, this one-dimensional approach is insufficient and in many ways it only further complicates the discourse. Payal Ahuja is a *bhārata nāṭyam* dancer who pursued a master's degree in dance studies at Roehampton in London and the Nalada Academy in Mumbai. She writes about her reaction to the methods of historical interpretation at in a western institution versus those at her school in Mumbai:

> As someone who has now been exposed to both approaches, that of dance studies in India and the UK, I find myself a little confused, as I seem to be caught between at least two different histories of the dance...In my opinion, the cultural history that we study at Nalada [beginning with the *nāṭya śāstra* and treats the tradition as cohesive over thousands of years] is as important as the modern history we are exposed to at Roehampton [nineteenth century onwards, specifically the revival period of *bhārata nāṭyam*]. But how are we to juxtapose these two perspectives when we in India do not have access to knowledge sources such as western publications? (Ahuja 2010, 112)

Acknowledging that one simple history is not enough, what kinds of frameworks are suited to groups that are built on multiple historical interpretations, all of which are considered valid? Speaking from the *bhārata nāṭyam* of her studies, Janet O'Shea warns that "none of the histories that practitioners put forth is spurious: dancers describe different versions of the past through the selection of competing sources, each of which constitutes a potentially valid historical 'truth'" (O'Shea 2006, 125). In the *oḍisī* field of music and dance, David Dennen notes that it is not the question of whether musical claims to authenticity in terms of adherence to classical texts or specific lineages are "true," but rather what is at stake is the "rhetorical force in an Indian context" of such claims (Dennen 2010, 150).

In all of the dance forms highlighted in the film, schools and lineages have been created and nurtured based on a certain history. Although these historical memories will depend on the lineages, regions, and individual preference, many times there are overlapping emphases across styles. Many schools and gurus will acknowledge a textual past, linking their tradition to such pan-Indian texts as the *Nāṭya Śāstra* and the *Abhinaya Darpaṇa*, in addition to regional textual sources. Some schools will promote links to the devotional temple dance traditions of their regions, but sometimes using what has become a pan-Indian term *devadāsī* instead of the regional equivalent. Dancers will also often measure their sense of history and classicism according to their teacher (*guru*), linking their guru with either or both of the textual or temple narratives. During the revival period of *bhārata nāṭyam*, two prominent dance figures from different communities (one, a traditional dancer from a *devadāsī* family, the other a western-educated, *brahmin* dancer) each claimed a history for the revived dance form – one held that the form had been nurtured by the *devadāsī* communities and the other that the form had roots farther back in the *Nāṭya Śāstra*. According to Janet O'Shea, these histories were mutually exclusive and dancers from these revival teachers were schooled in these separate histories and were later passed down and further expounded upon by their students.

Nina Dash, Sujata Mohapatra, and Kavitha Konda are all connected to forms that they perceive to have hardly changed from the temple period of their dance styles. Gautham Reddy, a PhD student in South Asia studies at the University of Chicago, in an interview not included in the final film, described his relationship to dance as not being historically aware at all until he stopped dancing and went to graduate school, at which point he learned about the *devadāsī* history within his style of *bhārata nāṭyam* (Reddy 2010). Before he academically learned about this specific historical past of his style, he still understood it as 'classical' but devoid of any kind of devotional history or practice. One trend is clear though - these terms link together past and present in an ongoing creative dialogue. These links to the texts and temple histories connect the contemporary dancers to a kind of *classical*, *traditional*, and *authentic* marker and in turn create a historically classical precedent for that dance form thus *creating* a specific classical history for their dance. *Classical-traditional-authentic* are terms that imply a certain kind of history, not simply adjectives that provide an aesthetic value judgment. But given the multiplicity of narratives, can we then still say that *bhārata nāṭyam, oḍiśī*, and *andhra nāṭyam* have one singular definition as *classical* Indian dances? Purnima Shah, in her paper on regional and national identities in Indian dance, and in the documentary film interview, notes that the Sangeet Natak Akademi, that awards titles of "classical" to art forms, has not published its criteria for or definition of classical (Shah 2002, 2010). So without any authoritative definition of what classicism is in this context, each style has had to define itself locally, nationally, and internationally as 'classical.' But then which history and what aesthetic metrics does that title imply?

In reaction to her dance background and scholarly training in the history of *bhārata nāṭyam*, O'Shea invokes the concept of "interpretive communities" to frame these divergent multiple histories. She writes:

> South Indian dance-style communities diverge in their interpretations of such concepts as authority, authenticity, and history...Authenticity... implies a sense of traditionalism which is rooted in a notion of history. The differing interpretive communities that constitute the different styles have come to define authenticity and tradition in varying ways, by creating images of the history and origins of the dance form, for example, and by referring to different historical moments as the source of the dance form. (O'Shea 1998, 51-52)

O'Shea does not go into too much detail on the idea of interpretive communities applied to this context, but she does emphasize that the two streams of dance communities I mentioned previously (the traditional dancer from a *devadāsī* family, the other a western-educated, *brahmin* dancer) are ones that have exclusively formed two fairly distinct sub-styles of the *bhārata nāṭyam*, both authentic and classical, both with their own origin histories (O'Shea 1998, 57). The "interpretive communities" framework that O'Shea cites is a useful one in the sense that it is a method of historical interpretation that allows for each community to have a valid historical understanding, but in her usage of the concept it does not allow for the acknowledgement of classicality and tradition across lineage of stylistic lines.

Many of the narratives I was treated to in this project do not fall along such clear cut lines of history as those in O'Shea's *bhārata nāṭyam* study. Even in my interviews with *bhārata nāṭyam* dancers, narratives of history varied significantly and overlapped style and lineage boundaries. Mythili Prakash, a very prominent internationally recognized *bhārata nāṭyam* dancer, even admitted to not following lineage boundaries in her professional life as a dancer (Prakash 2010). The modern forms of these classical dances share common narratives and important differences. These commonalities with differences complicate the interpretive communities model as outline by Stanley Fish and cited by Janet O'Shea. In his introduction to a work based on the model, Fish explains that it is the common background of each community that allows for mutual understanding and agreement, "[M]embers of the same [interpretive] community will necessarily agree because they will see (and by seeing, make) everything in relation to that community's assumed purposes and goals" (Fish 1980, 15). But even within one *lineage* tradition, as is the case of the *oḍiśī* dancers in my film, there is some disagreement, or more mildly, difference in focus and definition. Fish writes that his interpretive communities are "made up of those who share interpretive strategies not for reading but for writing texts, for constituting their properties" (Fish 1980, 14). While that may be the case for the very limited, very exclusive schools and lineages that do exist, it does not account for any sharing of interpretive understandings of classicality, authenticity, or the values that historical ties to ancient texts may produce across stylistic boundaries – across communities. How can these different lineages and

29

dance styles all acknowledge each other as classical and recognize all the varying histories as part of an overall classical dance tradition of India?

5. Publics, Memory, and Public Memory – A Framework for Classical Indian Dance Communities

The public memory of the classical history of Indian dance is part personal story, part factual history, and informed entirely through the lens of both the individual and the public itself - and it is the sharing of this memory that forms this public. In his book on the *bhakti* saint Namdev, Christian Novetzke explores the usage of 'public memory' over time to describe the history of remembrance of the saint in India. Namdev is remembered far beyond his homeland in western India and by many more people outside his traditional community and it is likely that competing narratives and historical memories exist in each community. Novetzke's purpose is not to find a historical Namdev or locate which of the histories that claim him are more accurate, but he is actually interested in the *idea* of Namdev and the "historical maintenance of his memory" (Novetzke 2008, 3). In many ways, Novetzke's framework for understanding the memory of the *bhakti* saint helps me understand the cultural construction of the many pasts of Indian dance. Without necessitating a chronological cultural history of any one form or the forms as a whole, the focus in oral narratives on the *ideas* of tradition, classicism, and authenticity rather than the historical *bhārata nāṭyam, oḍiśī*, etc. offers a tantalizing answer to Payal Ahuja's confusion. A public memory approach may also provide a more satisfying framework than separate interpretive communities that cannot take on the overlapping differences and continuities in such discursive communities. After reviewing Novetzke's understanding of public memory, I will unpack the terms *public* and *memory* from his work and outline how they fit into the case of Indian dance and then how the concept of public memory can help to draw out new concepts of historical narratives for these communities of artists.

Novetzke defines public memory as "the preservation of a past full of sentiment and historical sense maintained by religious communities" (Novetzke 2008, 2).[1] The purpose of his study is to investigate a number of "modes of remembrance" in order to "see how these activities constitute a practice that creates a dialogue between the past and the present and how this dialogue in turn constructs publics of reception in time" (2). Just as history, as communities imagine it, is an important part of the way Namdev *bhakti* communities understand vital aspects of their traditions, the negotiation of the past – that occurs in classrooms and performances in India and the diaspora – is also vital to acts of historical remembrance in 'classical' Indian dance forms. While Novetzke does not seek the requirement of modernity to understand publics or memory in his study, I would argue that this kind of historical memory in 'classical' Indian dance publics is created only in modernity. The thrust of a former colony into a nation state and cultural regions into states, all seeking new identities and carving out their own narratives, in addition to the more recent movements of these arts out of South Asia, form a public that is built on modernity but ever in a dialogue with the past. Janet O'Shea argues that you would not find this reflexive, self-conscious negotiation of historical memory in older dance forms and that it exists only in modern forms of classical dance, specifically for her *bhārata nāṭyam* (O'Shea 2007, 27). The notion of a "dialogue between past and present" that is continuous and constructive provides a broader base from which to view the acts of remembrance than that of the interpretive

---

[1] The problem of attempting to label classical Indian dancers as necessarily religious or non-religious is a very tricky proposition. In the film, Neha Limaye and Anjali Vora say that they do not have a religious connection to the dance and are generally non-religious. Mythili Prakash says that she is spiritual, but not religious and that in the context of classical dance, religious can be a physical act alone. Even so they still perform their *bhūmī namaskāram* before every dance and practice and perform religious pieces in temples. The problem of framing a definition of religiosity by speech acts is that it excludes practice and material culture in terms of what defines religious practice (Morgan 2010). This issue in classical Indian dance forms is complicated and out of the scope of this paper, but would be an excellent topic for future study. Here, although many of the dancers interviewed do find some kind of religious connection to the dance, I do not want to simply imply that all dancers are, thus in applying Novetzke's definition, I would leave out the qualifier "religious" in the definition of public memory.

community model, which at first glance does not posit more than a static community of interpretation and a single narrative.

Novetzke's model of a public memory is heavily influenced by both Michael Warner (publics) and Jan Assmann (memory). Instead of using a definition of *public* that requires ties to the state, Novetzke's 'public' is a more inclusive definition, that of a "mode of social cohesion, temporally bounded, and united in its aim toward affective display" (Novetzke 2008, 14). To reflect the continuous and productive processes of this kind of public, Novetzke looks to Warner's specifically reflexive publics. He quotes Warner: "[A] public enables a reflexivity in the circulation of texts among strangers who become, by virtue of their reflexively circulating discourse, a social entity" (Warner, quoted in Novetzke 2008, 17). For 'classical' Indian dancers, the constant public acts of remembering how they define their tradition and its history – the acceptance of those narratives by a public, and then that public's act of reissuing the narrative through their own lens of memory in performative acts – requires a kind of hermeneutic where the dialectic nature of these narratives can define the community. This reflexive and discursive nature of a public actually allows for the inclusion of not only dancers, but also those dance enthusiasts who are familiar with the forms, language of dance, and historical narratives. These *rasikas* (the term the *Nāṭya Śāstra* uses to refer to an "informed audience," Shah 2002, 127), actually form a kind of sub-public within the larger, specifically classical, Indian dance (or music) public. They take part in the performative discourse of performances, lectures, and books written by dancers and create their own narratives in terms of books, lectures, critiques, or even academies of dance in the case of Nina Dash. These *rasikas* are not practitioners, but they are still an important part of the reflexive and productive nature of this particular public. In addition to *rasikas*, this broad definition of a public allows for each style to form a sub-public under the larger Indian dance umbrella public.

In the case of these publics, it is useful to remember that the *classical history* of these dance forms, which I reviewed in the first third of the paper, and the narratives, or memory as I will move to shortly, of that history do more than define the discourse of a public. The identification of dance forms as 'classical' has socio-political implications and defines them against other non-classical forms. In fact, these modern, 'classical' Indian dance forms, taken as a public, can be seen as adopting identities and performing histories of classicism in relation to others. These dance forms are compared against other regional forms for the position of what is authentic and truly 'classical,' and they are commonly globally identified as classical against forms of dance such as ballet. In her study of the Marwari community in Calcutta, Anne Hardgrove speaks of relational publics and the fact that in their existence as a public, that the "Marwaris... needed somebody to be Marwari at" (Hardgrove 2004, 21). Purnima Shah writes about the creation of national and regional identities and narratives for these modern dance forms during the early post-independence period and their connection to the *Nāṭya Śāstra*:

> The urge to "elevate" various regional forms of performance to the status of the "classical" reflected the institutionalized desire for the regional communities to rebuild and take pride in their regional and national identity [post-indepenence]... Natyasastra therefore becomes one such emblem that reinstates "Indianness," integrating the diverse regional forms into more or less unified national forms. (Shah 2002, 138; Dennen 2010; and for an extensive discussion see Peterson and Soneji 2008)

In part of our interview not featured in the film, Professor Shah speaks also about the post-colonial independence pressures on Indian dance forms to become classical, but of course classical in relation to an international idea of classicism:

> You can lay down points after points after points about what is it that makes something classic. So yes these ["classical" Indian] forms do meet with some of those [western] criteria, but the main important thing to understand in terms of Indian dance was that it was during the period when India has just become independent and it has nothing to bank on. It was state of chaos...so there was not very much available to the people – but culture was something that the upper echelons of the political society thought: that is something that we can create. Now India needs to be identified as India – as an independent India – we are no longer British...

> So to create this independent identity, the government came up with three academies... [music/dance/theater, visual arts, literature arts, of which Sangeet Natak Akademi is one]and these academies were responsible to go back into the past and recreate that golden period of literature [being one example], bring all of that literature into today's context, popularize that literature, and generate new literature based on that. (Shah 2010)

After *bhārata nāṭyam*'s international success, however, other regional dance forms, such as *āndhra nāṭyam* and *oḍiśī*, also had to become classical in relation to that form and its conception of classicism (also in Shah 2002, 138).

So far I have yet to define what exactly memory implies in the context of these dance communities or how it is enacted.[2] This interpretation of the function of memory in the formation of a public is taken again from Novetzke's public memory, but the underlying social requirement of memory and publics comes from a Durkheimian understanding of public memory. The Durkheimian angle comes from an inherently social basis for public memory through Warner and more specifically Jan Assmann's concept of a memory that can be socially "connective" (Novetzke 2008, 25-26; Phillips 2004; Assmann 2006). Novetzke writes,"[P]ublics, by their nature, remember and are constituted by a shared memory. Indeed...publics are systems of memory" (Novetzke 2008, 18). He writes that these publics, "are ruled neither by dogma nor coercion, but made cohesive by a kind of social agreement that has a precedent in the genealogy of *bhakti*" (18). For the classical dance publics, the boundaries of the public are not formed by membership in a specific lineage or school but in this "social agreement" of a kind of genealogy of classicism.

---

[2] Although this study is concerned with only *inclusive memory*, of critical importance to the study of public memory in classical Indian dance publics is the concept of forgetting. In our film interview, Purnima Shah notes that many dancers and teachers often pass over unsavory historical moments in their remembrances of historical narratives. She recalls that in her training as a *bhārata nāṭyam* dancer, "she never even heard the word *sadir*" (Shah 2010). These moments of forgetting or decisions to forget, influenced by social, political and cultural factors, can tell us as much or even more about the process of memory production and how memory performance affects the public and would serve as an extension of this kind of treatment.

Publics such as the Namdev *bhakti* public and the classical Indian dance public as a whole, but also sub-publics of lineages and *rasikas*, are "centered on the circulation of a common stock of memory and mnemonic practices and participation in the publics" (18). In the case of the classical dance public(s), there is a common language both in words and in movement across styles in addition to mnemonic practices ranging from the form of classroom or performative introduction in the dance forms, to the obeisance paid to the earth before a practice, to the very repertoire of each style. The use of these "memory and mnemonic practices and participations" form publics on various levels based on the inclusion of specific memories and practices. In the very detailed performance of these memories in terms of systematic movements, publics are formed in the local sense in lineages and regional styles, but at the same time the more general memories and mnemonic practices form a larger public that crosses style lines.

Novetzke leaves open the type of memory and mnemonic practices available to publics for their existence because of the fluid nature of memory and what memory can consist of and take place in:

> Such memories may be formalized histories or less logically structured modes of recollection; they might center on a site or an object, of a shared imagination, and the perpetuation of memory might be restricted to, or combined with, orality, literacy, visuality, ritual and so on. But publics must record themselves in order to be sustained even for the shortest duration – they must remember. (23)

The use of memory to interpret the historical narratives of dancers in these publics allows us to step back from a need to classify a set of narratives as valid or not and allows both of Payal Ahuja's histories to coexist as part of a greater discourse within that public. If the recasting of historical memories is the foundation of the formation of a public, we should ask how are these memories are actually enacted on a regular basis outside of the interview setting of this film. In his discussion of public memory, Edward Casey reminds the reader that among the many varied forms of memory and recollection, there also exists a "body memory" (Casey 2004, 21). The recognition of the body as being a site of memory and recollection can be broadened to include the body as a site of specific histories and narratives that have been cultivated through a public. Actual performances of these dance forms can be considered the visual and material manifestations of the negotiation of public memory for this kind of public. Purnima Shah has studied the national dance festivals that take place in India as sites of memory and active negotiation of those memories: "These festivals also function as national sites where social memory is evoked, and regional and national identities are negotiated and reformulated through the performance of regional dance forms" (Shah 2002, 126). Apart from the festivals acting as sites for these forms of memory, the actual constituent parts of dance performances and choreographic decisions also serve as moments and modes of memory within the public. Janet O'Shea defines choreography as a type of socio-political strategy:

> I defined choreography as the planned and intentional selection of movement that includes the arrangement of conventional items of repertoire, material generated through improvisation, and the composition of entirely new work. All of these forums offered dancers opportunities to express their perspectives on history, politics, and the social meanings of bharata natyam. (O'Shea 2006, 143)

Ramya Sundaresan Kapadia, in our film interview, says that she goes back to a classical text to ground new choreographic pieces, and then also to her gurus or other instructors (Kapadia 2010). In the choreographic process, dancers navigate histories and memories of their art forms. Ramya had studied at least two styles of *bhārata nāṭyam* and has been exposed to countless others. Her active consideration of *how* to choreograph an item reflects her conscious dialogue with memory in the act of adding to the discourse of the dance public. In terms of the actual body in which the "body memory" is instilled, Sujata Mohapatra discusses such a "trained body" in our film interview. When I asked her how she (and her lineage) keep the traditional *oḍiśī* "flavor" in performance items, she argued that once a dancer is properly trained, with all of what that means in terms of technical, devotional, and understanding of the style, the trained "body will not accept anything that is not authentic" (Mohapatra 2010). The memory of the boundaries of that tradition (i.e. historical decisions, memories of temple sculpture, etc.) become a part of the body memory, and so she argues that such an idealized trained body cannot be anything but classical.

If a dancer were to view the short film and then read this paper and feel utterly confused as to *what* the history of their style or lineage or 'classical' Indian dance is, I could understand the anxiety. I began this section with my own story and I have to admit that the story does not have an end where I can collectively gather my thoughts and cast a verdict on the history of my dance form (which actually includes all three of the dance styles highlighted in the film). An approach that begins with narratives and uses memory to frame them is by definition one that is based plurality. I am inspired by Hamilton and Shope's introduction to the usefulness of such a method when they see the field of memory studies and oral histories move from "*what* people remember, or the content of their interviews, to *why* they remember, or the meaning of people's recollections" (Hamilton and Shopes 2008, ix). By using an approach that allows for both an individual and a larger community to both actively engage a discourse, we can see how each affect the overarching narrative of that public. In the case of classical Indian dance, the use of public memory is broad enough to allow for the regional and national streams of memory to exist in sometimes concentric, sometimes overlapping circles of memory reproduction, performance, and reflection. The method also allows for the inclusion of the informed audience, *rasikas*, to form another sub-public that moves in and out of the other publics but still shares historical memories with the dance publics. Moving forward, this project serves to outline a new approach to studying these dance communities and cultural history projects, like Novetzke's, would be an obvious extension of this premise. Collections of essays such as *Performing Pasts*, edited by Indira Viswanathan Peterson and Davesh Soneji, offer interesting new avenues for the study of pasts, classicism, and authority within the arts in modern South Asia, however, I believe the

38

scholarship on classical Indian dance and music could benefit from this kind of project. A study in oral histories and public memory that looks towards the maintenance of the perceived public memory, not only what is included and excluded as canonical, traditional, classical, and authentic within that public, would add both the narrow and the broad negotiations of past in modern art forms and look towards how they are actively sustained in modern socio-political and cultural contexts.

References

Ahuja, Payal. 2010. "Local/Global Histories of Bharatnatyam." In *Dance Matters: Performing India,* edited by Pallabi Chakravorty and Nilanjana Gupta, 108-13. New York: Routledge.

Allen, Matthew. 1997. "Rewriting the Script for South Indian Dance." *The Drama Review* Journal of Performance Studies 41 (3): 63-100.

Assmann, Jan. 2006. *Religion and Cultural Memory*. Translated by Rodney Livingstone. Stanford: Stanford University Press.

Bakhle, Janaki. 2005. *Two Men and Music: Nationalism, Colonialism and the Making of an Indian Classical Tradition*. Oxford: Oxford University Press.

Bayer, Julia, Andrea Engl, and Melanie Liebheit. 2004. "Du- ka's Dilemma—Ethnologischer Film im Fernsehen. Ein Gespräch mit Jean Lydall und Werner Dütsch." In Strategien der Annäherung. Darstellungen des Fremden im deutschen Fernsehen, edited by Julia Bayer, Andrea Engl, and Melanie Liebheit, 78-98. München: Horlemann.

Casey, Edward S. 2004."Public Memory in Place and Time." In *Framing Public Memory*, edited by Kendall R. Phillips, 1-17. Tuscaloosa: The University of Alabama Press.

"Classical," *The Oxford English Dictionary Online*, accessed February 27, 2011, http://oxforddictionaries.com/view/entry/m_en_us1233539#m_en_us1233539.

Clifford, James. 1983. "On Ethnographic Authority." *Representations* 1(2): 118-146.

Dash. Nileena (Nina). Personal Interview. 26 September 2010.

Dasmuth, Parijata. Personal Interview. 27 Sept. 2009.

Dennen, David. 2010. "The Third Stream: Oḍiśī Music, Regional Nationalism, and the Concept of "Classical."" *Asian Music* 41.2: 149-179.

Dwibedi, Kavita. *Odissi Lecture Demonstration*. University of Hyderabad, Hyderabad, Andhra Pradesh. 10 August 2010. Lecture Demonstration.

Fish, Staley. 1980. *Is there a text in this class? The Authority of Interpretive Communities*. Cambridge: Harvard University Press.

Gaston, Anne-Marie. 1996. *Bharata Natyam From Temple to Theatre*. New Delhi: Manohar Publishers.

Geroy, Amanda. Personal Interview. 26 September 2010.

Hamilton, Paula, and Linda Shopes. 2008. "Introduction: Building Partnerships between Oral History and Memory Studies." *Oral Histories and Public Memories*, edited by Paula Hamilton and Linda Shopes, Philadelphia: Temple University Press.

Hardgrove, Anne. 2004. *Community and Public Culture:The Marwaris in Calcutta, c. 1897-1997*. New York: Columbia University Press.

Kapadia, Ramya Sundaresan. Personal Interview. 11 October 2010.

Kersenboom-Story, Saskia. 1987. *Nityasumangali: Devadasi Tradition in South India*. Delhi: Motilal Banarsidass.

Konda, Kavitha. Personal Interview. 1 October 2010.

Kothari, Sunil. Informal Presentation. Residence of Nileena Dash. 29, September 2009. House Lecture.

Levin, Melinda C., and Alicia Re Cruz. 2008. "Behind the Scenes of a Visual Ethnography: A Dialogue between Anthropology and Film." *Journal of Film and Video* 60.2: 59-68.

Loizos, Peter. 1992. "Admissible Evidence? Film in Anthropology." In *Film as Ethnography*, edited by Peter Ian Crawford and David Turton, 50-65. Manchester: Manchester University Press.

Lydall, Jean. 2008. "Intimacy, Integrity, and Indulgence in Anthropological Film." *Journal of Film and Video* 60.2: 35-49.

Meduri, Avanthi. 1988. "Bharatha Natyam – What Are You?" *Asian Theatre Journal* 5.1: 1-22.

Mills, Margaret. 1991. *Rhetoric and Politics in Afghan Traditional Storytelling* Philadelphia: University of Pennsylvania Press.

Misztal, Barbara. 2003. *Theories of Social Remembering*. Berkshire: Open University Press.

Mohapatra, Sujata. Personal Interview. 18 November 2010.

Morgan, David. 2010. "Introduction: The Matter of Belief." In *Religion and Material Culture: The Matter of Belief*, edited by David Morgan, 1-18. New York: Routledge.

Narayan, Kirin. 1993. "How Native is a "Native" Anthropologist?" *American Anthropologist* 95.3: 671-686.

Novetzke, Christian Lee. 2007. "*Bhakti* and its Public" *International Journal of Hindu Studies* 11.3: 255-272.

---. 2008. *Religion and Public Memory: A Cultural History of Saint Namdev in India*. New York: Columbia University Press.

O'Shea, Janet. 2007. *At Home in the World: Bharata Natyam on the Global Stage*. Middletown: Wesleyan University Press.

---. 2006. "Dancing Through History and Ethnography: Indian Classical Dance and the Performance of the Past." In *Dancing from Past to Present: Nation, Culture, Identities*, edited by Theresa Jill Buckland, 123-149. Madison: University of Wisconsin Press.

---. 1998. "Traditional" Indian Dance and the Making of Interpretive Communities" *Asian Theatre Journal*. 15.1: 45-63.

Peterson, Indira Viswanathan, and Davesh Soneji. 2008. eds. *Performing Pasts: Reinventing the Arts in Modern South India*. New Delhi: Oxford University Press.

Phillips, Kendall R. ed. 2004. *Framing Public Memory*. Tuscaloosa: The University of Alabama Press.

Prasad, Leela. 2007. *Poetics of Conduct: Oral Narrative and Being in a South Indian Town*. New York: Columbia University Press.

Prakash, Mythili. Personal Interview. 24 October 2010.

Reddy, Gautham. Personal Interview. 19 October 2010.

Shah, Purnima. Personal Interview 8 October 2010.

---. 2002. "State Patronage in India: Appropriation of the 'Regional' and 'National.'" *Dance Chronicle* 25.1: 125-141.

"Shastra/śāstra," *Monier Williams Sanskrit-English Dictionary,* accessed February 27, 2011, http://www.sanskrit-lexicon.uni-koeln.de/monier/.

Soneji, Davesh, ed. 2010. *The Bharatanatyam Reader*. Oxford: Oxford University Press.

Warner, Michael. 2002. *Publics and Counterpublics*. New York: Zone Books.

Weidman, Amanda J. 2006. *Singing the Classical, Voicing the Modern: The Post-Colonial Politics of Music in South India*. Durham: Duke University Press.

CPSIA information can be obtained
at www.ICGtesting.com
Printed in the USA
LVIC04n1519070114
368461LV00019B/100

* 9 7 8 1 2 4 8 9 4 5 3 6 0 *